Weather

Fiona Macdonald

FRANKLIN WATTS
A Division of Grolier Publishing
NEW YORK • LONDON • HONG KONG • SYDNEY
DANBURY, CONNECTICUT

Series editor: Helen Lanz
Series designer: John Christopher, WHITE DESIGN
Picture research: Sue Mennell
Illustrators: Peter Bull, Carolyn Scrace and Sarah John
Consultant: Dot Jackson

First published in by Franklin Watts

First American edition 2000 by Franklin Watts
A Division of Grolier Publishing
90 Sherman Turnpike
Danbury, CT 06816

Visit Franklin Watts/Chilren's Press on the Internet at:
http://publishing.grolier.com

A catalog record for this title is available from the
Library of Congress

ISBN: 0-531-14544-1 (lib.bdg.)   0-531-15428-9 (pbk.)

Picture credits

Cover: Image Bank/John P. Kelly (inset); Still Pictures/Kent Wood (main image)

Interior Pictures:
Illustrations: Peter Bull: 4, 6, 8t, 9 (both), 11, 17t, 20, 21, 25; Carolyn Scrace 14-15, 16; Sarah John: 8b, 10, 15b, 18, 29
Photography: Bruce Coleman 9 ((Staffan Widstrand), 231 (Orion Press), 23r (John Shaw), 24 (Kim Taylor), 25 (Dr Eckart Pott), 26 (Alain Compost); (Steve Shott); Dylan Garcia 21b; Robert Harding 11l, 21t (Ron Oulds); Photodisc 12b, 14, 28; Science Photo Library 5 (NASA); Still Pictures 7t (Ron Giling), 7b (NASA), 11r (Hartmut Schwarzbach), 13b (Dibble-UNEP) 16 (Hjalte Tin), 19 (Keith Kent); The StockMarket 12t (B. Harris), 22r (A & J Verkaik), 27 (Lester Lefkowitz); SkyScan 22 (both left).

Acknowledgments: page 10: Sunflakes by Frank Asch, Country Pie, 1979, by permission of Greenwillow Books, a Division of William Morrow & Co.
Every effort has been made to gain permission to reproduce the following poem: page 15: The Cloud Mobile by Mary Swenson, from Nature: Poems Old and New published by Houghton Mifflin, © Saint Martin's Press.

Contents

Weather Around the World

Wherever we live in the world, the weather influences our lives. Sun, rain, wind, and snow affect the houses we build, the foods we can grow, what we wear, and what we do each day. Some people say that the weather also affects our health and our moods.

Polar

Temperate

Tropical

Temperate

Polar

Three Main Climate Zones:

Tropical:	Hot and wet for most of the year.
Temperate:	Mild and rainy; four separate seasons.
Polar:	Very cold for most of the year.

Smaller Climate Zones:

Subtropical:	Hot, fairly wet, but long dry season.
Arid:	Very dry; hot in daytime, cold at night.
Semi-arid:	Hot days, cool nights, fairly dry.
Mediterranean:	Hot, dry summers; cool wet winters.
Northern temperate:	Mild summers; cold, long, rainy winters.
Mountain:	Cold and snowy.

Climate Zones

There are three main climate zones in the world: tropical (hot and wet), temperate (mild and rainy), and polar (cold and snowy).

The weather within these main zones can vary a lot, especially where there are mountains, or where land is beside the sea. Because of this, there are smaller climate zones within the three main zones.

◀ *You can see the main climate zones and the smaller climate zones on this map.*

Weather Words

Many different words are used to describe weather. Some weather words are listed below. See if you can find them and discover what they mean as you read through this book:

climate

meteorologist

satellite

temperature

cumulus

forecast

tornado

El Niño

Try This! Weather Zones

▲ *This satellite picture of the earth, taken from space, is colored according to temperature. Red and deep red shows the hottest areas; pink shows the next hottest, then yellow. Warm oceans are shown as light blue; cold oceans are dark blue.*

Use this photograph and the world map (see *page 4*) to create your own picture of the world's climate zones.

Instead of using different colors to show the different temperatures of each zone, you could draw people wearing the most appropriate clothing for the zone they are in. For example, if you were in a polar climate, you would need to be wrapped up very warm.

Or you could make up a key for each zone, like the weather symbols you see on the weather forecast.

Very Hot, Very Cold

The world's weather has temperatures that can range from very hot to very cold. Temperature is measured with a thermometer. It is usually measured in one of two units — Fahrenheit or Celsius.

Fahrenheit and Celsius

In 1714, the German scientist Gabriel Fahrenheit developed a scale for measuring temperature. He based it on two things he had noticed: the freezing point and the boiling point of water. He called the freezing point of water 32°F and the boiling point 212°F.

In 1742, the Swedish astronomer Anders Celsius invented a new scale. This was improved five years later by the Swedish scientist Carolus Linnaeus. The Celsius scale is based on the freezing point of water being 0°C and the boiling point 100°C.

Number Work

Use the thermometer on this page to help work out these problems. You can give your answers in °F or °C.

✪ **What is the difference between the world's hottest average temperature of 94°F (34.4°C) and the world's coldest average temperature of -72°F (-57.8°C) .**

✪ **What is the difference between the highest temperature ever recorded 136°F (57.8°C) and the lowest temperature ever recorded -128.6°F (-89.2°C).**

✪ **Make up some more temperature puzzles of your own and give them to a friend to solve.**

◄ *Mathematicians and scientists find the Celsius, or Centigrade, scale much easier to use than the Fahrenheit scale.*

Did you know...

The highest temperature ever recorded on earth was 136°F (57.8°C) in Libya, North Africa.

The country with the hottest weather year-round is Ethiopia, also in Africa. The average temperature there is 94°F (34.4°C) .

The coldest temperature ever measured was -128.6°F -(89.2°C) in Antarctica.

Antarctica is also the coldest continent year-round. The average temperature there is -72°F (-57.8°C).

🔺 *It is very difficult to grow crops in the hot, dry climate of Ethiopia.*

🔺 *Antarctica is one of the windiest, as well as coldest, places on earth.*

Feeling the Heat

We have learned how to live in many different environments, but we can suffer if temperatures rise or fall too much.

At around 90°F (32°C) people start to feel very hot and sticky. At 106°F (41°C) we begin to feel unwell. Temperatures above that can be dangerous, because the body starts to overheat.

We also suffer at low temperatures. Without clothes, we feel cold at 68°F (20°C).

Temperature is affected by the wind. We feel colder if the wind is blowing.

Keeping Hot, Keeping Cold

Materials that don't allow heat or cold to pass through are called insulators. Insulators keep our bodies from losing heat and from becoming too cold.

This experiment will help you find out which materials are the best insulators, and why.

YOU CAN TRY THIS!

Insulators Part One

You will need:

- plastic bag filled with ice
- clothespin
- hot water bottle (get an adult to help you with this)
- pen and paper

ASK AN ADULT

- piece of aluminum foil
- paper
- cotton wool pad
- piece of plastic bubble wrap
- cotton garment (such as a T-shirt)
- woolen garment (such as a sweater)

Cold
Good and bad insulators

Material	Score
Foil	
Paper	
Cotton Wool	
Bubble wrap	
Cotton garment	
Woolen garment	

1 Use the clothespin to attach the different materials to the plastic bag as shown.

2 Gently touch each item in turn.

3 Which feels the coldest?

Give each material a score out of 10.
Give 10 for the most cold; 1 for the least cold.

4 Write down your scores in a chart (see left).

If you can feel the cold through the material, it is not a good insulator. It is allowing the heat from your hand to pass through to the ice in the bag.

Insulators Part Two

1 Repeat the experiment using the hot water bottle instead of the bag of ice.

2 Give each material a score. Give 10 for the most heat you can feel through the material and 1 for the least heat.

3 Write down your scores in a chart.

The materials that let through the least heat are the best insulators. Put the materials in order, listing them from the best insulator (lowest number) to the worst (highest number).

? **Look closely at your lowest-scoring materials. What are they like?**

You will probably find that the plastic bubble wrap and the sweater worked best as insulators. This is because they both trap air inside or beneath their layer. Air is very good insulator.

Trapped Air

Skin

Material

▶ Wearing many layers of clothes allows people to survive in temperatures as low as -76°F (-60°C).

A Lot of Hot Air!

The right clothes can insulate people from the dangerous effect of extreme heat or cold. In hot climates people wear long, loose clothes that leave room for air to circulate inside. In cold climates people wear many layers of clothes to trap air in between the layers and keep in the body heat.

The Changing Seasons

In many parts of the world, the weather patterns change several times a year. These regular weather patterns are called seasons.

We expect the weather to behave in certain ways in each season.

Winter is the coldest season; summer is the hottest. Spring and autumn are usually somewhere in between.

Try This! Sunflakes

If sunlight fell like snowflakes,
gleaming yellow and so bright,
we could build a sunman,
we could have a sunman fight,
we could watch the sunflakes
drifting in the sky.

We could go sleighing
in the middle of July
through sundrifts and sunbanks,
we could ride a sunmobile,
and we could touch sunflakes –
I wonder how they'd feel.

FRANK ASCH

Try writing a poem about other weather in this way, such as fog flakes or snow beams.

Winter is the coldest season. Days are often wet and foggy. There is often snow and ice.

Spring can be wet and windy, with some warmer, sunny days.

Summer is the hottest season. But there can be thunderstorms and heavy rain, as well as hot, sunny days.

Autumn can bring frosty mornings, with cooler days and nights. The days can be sunny, but not always hot.

The Reason for Seasons

Seasons occur because of the way the earth orbits (moves around) the sun.

The earth is tilted at an angle: different parts of the earth get different amounts of heat and light at different times of the year.

As the earth moves around the sun, the part tilted towards the sun gets more heat and light from the sun's rays. It has summer.

The part tilted away from the sun gets less heat and light, and so it has winter.

Sun

Did you know...

The Northern Hemisphere (the northern half of the earth) is tilted toward the sun between April and September when northern countries, such as the U.S. and Canada, have their summer.

The Southern Hemisphere (the southern half of the earth) is tilted away from the sun between April and September. Southern countries, such as Australia and New Zealand, have their winter at this time.

Season Festivals

People around the world celebrate the changing seasons in different ways.

◀ *In India, men dance and play music in the street as part of the spring festival.*

▲ *A masked dancer at an autumn festival in Tibet.*

Weather Forecasts

In the past there were no scientific weather forecasts, but people still needed to know what weather conditions to expect. Like today, farmers needed to know when the weather would be favorable for sowing or harvesting their crops. Sailors wanted to steer clear of dangerous storms at sea.

▶ This weather radar helps make modern weather forecasts much more accurate than forecasts in the past.

Try This!

Be a natural weather forecaster. Test these old-fashioned ways of foretelling the weather to find out if they work.

Find a pine cone or, if you can get to the seashore, a strip of seaweed. Hang either one up outdoors, in a sheltered place.

When the air is moist (a sign of approaching rain), the pine cone will close up and the seaweed will feel limp and slimy.

When the air is dry (a sign of clear weather), the pine cone will open and the seaweed will feel stiff and leathery.

Weather Watchers

Today, scientists called meteorologists study the weather. They use radar to monitor rain and snow. Weather balloons and satellites give us information about clouds and storms. All this information is automatically radioed to weather stations on the ground.

At the weather stations, meteorologists analyze the information to help them predict weather patterns. However, they don't always get it right!

Did you know...

Weather balloons carry instruments that take temperature readings high above the earth.

Radar is a system for finding the positions of objects in the air. Heavy rain, thunderstorms, hurricanes, and tornadoes show up on radar. It sends out radio waves that bounce back off clouds or storms.

Weather satellites orbit the earth. They send back pictures of how clouds are forming.

◀ Satellites, such as this one, are very powerful. The images they send back give us a lot of information (see page 5).

Weather Sayings

Before modern technology, people learned to predict weather patterns by watching nature.

They made up sayings to help them remember what they had found out.

A sunshiny shower
Won't last an hour.

Clear moon,
Frost soon.

◀ Some sayings are true. A cold, frosty morning often follows a bright, clear moonlit night. But when the moon is surrounded by clouds, damp, stormy weather often follows the next day.

Clouds

The air around us contains water, although we cannot usually see it. This water comes from the sea, rivers, and lakes.

When the sun heats up water on the surfaces of the sea, rivers, and lakes, it evaporates and turns into a gas called water vapor. In the air, the water vapor becomes tiny droplets of water.

The clouds we see floating in the sky are made of these water droplets. When clouds rise very high above the earth's surface, they cool down and the water droplets turn into crystals of ice.

Clouds form in many different shapes and sizes.

Different clouds are often linked to different types of weather.

Cirrus clouds form high in the sky, where it is coldest.

Delicate altocumulus clouds are signs of approaching gales.

Stratus clouds are large, low clouds that often lead to drizzle.

Huge cumulonimbus clouds bring thunderstorms.

Meteorologists can tell a lot by studying the formation of clouds.

OBILE

*Do you know what the poem is describing?
Look at this picture to help you figure it out.*

Above my face is a map.
Continents form and fade.
Blue countries, made
on a white sea, are erased,
and white countries traced
on a blue sea.

MAY SWENSON

Try This! Make a Cloud Mobile

YOU CAN TRY THIS!

You will need:
- **white cardboard**
- **white or clear thread**
- **adhesive tape**
- **black coloring pencil**
- **lengths of plastic tube or bamboo**

1 Using the pictures on these pages to help you, draw and cut out the different types of clouds. Shade the dark clouds with the black coloring pencil.

2 Fix lengths of thread to each of your cut-outs with tape.

3 Hang each cloud from a different length of wire. Use the picture on page 14 to get each different type of cloud at the right height.

4 Attach the clouds to a plastic tube or bamboo to make a mobile. You will have to move the thread on the tube or bamboo to make it balance.

⬆ *Hang your mobile where the clouds have plenty of room to move.*

Rain

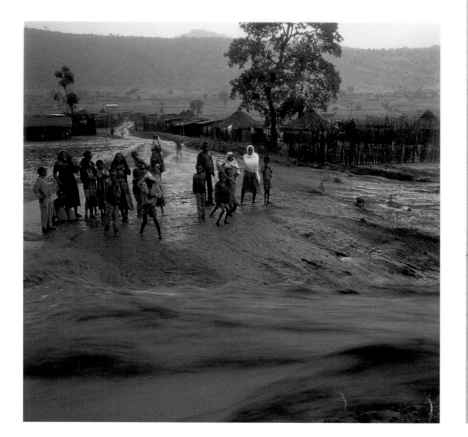

These people in Ethiopia gather to watch floodwaters rage past their village, after two years of drought.

Over the centuries rain has been welcomed and feared. It has brought life-giving water to people, animals, and plants. It has also caused terrible floods, sweeping away houses, covering roads, and ruining crops in waterlogged fields.

Rain forms when tiny water droplets in clouds combine and make bigger, heavier drops that fall to the ground.

Different types of clouds produce different types of rainfall. Flat sheets of stratus clouds (*see page 14*), which cover a wide area, produce long periods of rain. Fluffy-looking cumulus clouds, which are surrounded by blue sky, produce short showers.

Rainmakers

Throughout history, people have held special ceremonies and said prayers to try to make rain fall.

In medieval Europe, witches threatened to create storms against people who annoyed them. They claimed to have wind and rain tied up in their handkerchiefs.

In ancient America, the Hopi people held rain dances to try to end droughts.

Native Americans living on the Great Plains prayed to the Thunderbird, who brought rain.

Did you know...

Raindrops fall in many different sizes. The smallest are only $2/100$ in (0.5 mm) across. The largest can be $1/4$ in (6.5 mm) wide.

Make a Rain Measure

1 *Cut the top off the bottle.*

2 *Use a waterproof pen and ruler to mark inches (centimeters) up the side of the bottle.*

3 *Place the cut-off bottle top upside down over the main part of the bottle, to make a funnel.*

4 *Place the bottle on a flat piece of ground away from overhanging buildings or trees.*

5 *Observe the rainwater level every day; record it in your notebook, then pour the rainwater away.*

You will need:
- plastic bottle
- scissors
- waterproof pen
- ruler
- notebook and pen

Try to keep rainfall records every day for a month. You can record your findings on a bar chart. Choose the week in which you had the most rain. Put the days of the week along the bottom axis of the bar chart. Put inches (centimeters) along the vertical side of the chart. Draw in your results for that week (see the chart to the left to help you).

 Did it rain every day? Which was the wettest day? How much rain fell?

17

Thunder and Lightning

Thunderstorms can happen anytime, and anywhere except Antarctica, where it is too cold. They occur most often in spring and summer, and in tropical regions (*see map, page 4*).

Electricity

Thunderstorms are caused by huge masses of warm air coming together in a cloud and rising high into the sky. The air inside the thundercloud rises and falls. Vast amounts of electricity build up inside it. No one knows exactly how this happens.

Electricity inside thunderclouds causes the air to expand (get larger) and make a booming sound, called thunder.

Electricity that jumps across thunderclouds or to the ground is called lightning.

...if it is red, there is rain in the air.

...if it is yellow, the air is dusty.

...if it is blue, it is hailing.

Lightning can be several different colors, depending on the air it travels through. If the lightning is white, then the air is dry...

Keep Safe in a Storm

Move indoors if possible, or get inside
a car or a bus.

Do not touch electrical equipment (including
telephones and computers) or water pipes.

If outdoors, stay away from anything metal,
like gates or fences.

Do not take shelter under lampposts,
signposts, or trees.

BEWARE

If your hair stands on end, this means
danger! Crouch close to the ground.

Do not look up or lie flat until the
storm has passed.

*Cloud-to-ground lightning
causes fires and can strike people.*

Wordgame

**Try to make at least 50
words from the letters in:**

T h u n d e r s t o r m

**Here are some to start
you off: thunder, storm,
store, under, mother,
drum...**

THOR AND THE MIDGARD SERPENT

According to ancient Viking legends, Thor, the god of thunder, rode through the sky in a chariot pulled by goats, smashing giant snakes with his mighty hammer and creating thunder and lightning. Thor was the favorite god of Viking peasants and farmers.

The Vikings lived their lives by the sea and were fearless sailors. They believed that the sea and waves were ruled by different gods. But violent storms at sea were caused by a huge and evil serpent — the serpent of Midgard. It lay beneath the waves and curled its enormous body around the world.

Thor hated the serpent. He was determined to kill it. He asked the giant fishermen, who knew where it lived, for help. One of the giants, Hymir, agreed.

Thor and Hymir set off in a small boat with an ox's head as bait. They reached the place where they believed the serpent to be. Thor fixed the ox's head to a giant hook attached to a thick, strong rope. He launched them into the sea and waited.

Suddenly the rope tightened; the sea turned black and began to churn. Thor quickly took up the rope. He pulled with all his strength, and as he pulled, the serpent's head rose from the stormy waves.

The serpent of Midgard, hooked by the tongue, realized the power of Thor. It wrapped its immense body around the rocks under the sea, but still it could not withstand Thor's great strength. As the tiring serpent fought, it spat its venom and flashed its fierce eyes.

Hymir, frightened and not realizing the serpent was weakening, could bear it no longer. He struck the rope with his axe. Thor fell back. The serpent sank below the waves before Thor could throw his hammer.

Thor could not believe what Hymir had done. In his rage, Thor cast Hymir into the depths of the sea.

The serpent recovered from its wounds. The Vikings believed that it continued to stir up stormy seas, causing many of their ships to be wrecked.

Wild Winds

Wind is moving air. Air moves because it is hotter or colder, wetter or drier, than other air nearby.

World Winds

Many different types of wind blow over the surface of the earth. You can see two of the most important ones in the diagram below.

Some winds feel wild and strong; others feel soft and gentle. Many winds blow in the same areas at the same time every year. They are so well known that they have names.

The Scirocco brings hot weather from Africa to southern Europe.

Monsoons bring rain to India in the summer.

Did you know...

Wind can provide energy. In the past, windmills (above) were used to grind corn. Today there are wind farms (below), where generators turn energy from the wind into electricity.

Swirling Storms

In hot, tropical regions, several large thunderstorms sometimes bunch together over the ocean. The massive clouds they contain swirl around and around. They form a huge wall, up to 9 mi (15 km) high, around an area of calm.

These swirling clouds begin to move across the ocean, getting faster all the time. They produce winds of more than 155 mph (250 kph). They create enormous amounts of rain — up to 24 in (600 mm) in one day. They cause massive waves called storm surges.

Tornadoes are terrifying funnel-shaped storms. They are one of the most dangerous types of weather. Tornadoes are formed when thunderclouds meet high-speed winds many miles above ground. Tall, twisting columns of air form inside the cloud and spin down to the ground. This causes a fierce whirlwind, rushing around and around at almost 310 mph (500 kph). It can snatch up heavy objects, such as cars, and can tear the roofs off buildings.

◀ This swirling storm, shown in black with the area of calm at the centre in white, is moving across the United States (left and below).

◀ This type of swirling storm is called a typhoon, cyclone or hurricane in different parts of the world.

Snow and Ice

Snow and ice are formed when water vapor in clouds falls to a temperature of 32°F (0°C) or below. Then the water vapor turns into crystals of ice. The ice crystals join together and become too heavy to float in the air. They fall to the ground as snowflakes.

▶ *Snowflakes are made up of ice crystals. The crystals combine to make beautiful patterns.*

◀ *These figures and buildings are larger than life — and all sculpted out of snow.*

Dangerous Beauty

Ice and snow look very beautiful and can be great fun to play in. But they can also be dangerous. Ice on roads makes driving very difficult. Huge snowfalls in mountain areas can cause snow to come crashing down the slopes as avalanches.

Never walk on frozen ponds or lakes; ice may look thick, but it can break easily underfoot.

! BEWARE

Snow Sculptures

Every year in February, the Japanese city of Sapporo holds a huge Snow Festival. Artists carve enormous statues, many times larger than life, out of tightly packed snow.

Weather Wonders

Sunlight, wind, water, and ice can create many magical weather effects.

Rainbows

Rainbows appear in showery weather. They are made when sunlight shines on water droplets in the sky. Sunlight looks clear and white, but it is made up of many different colors. Each water droplet splits up the sunlight into the different colors of the rainbow.

➥ *Rainbows are curved. The lower the sun is in the sky, the higher the rainbow arch will be.*

Wordgame

There are sayings to help people remember the colors of a rainbow. Have you heard the saying: Richard Of York Gave Battle In Vain?

The first letter of each word relates to a color. These are also the order the colors appear in the rainbow.

Richard	Red
Of	Orange
York	Yellow
Gave	Green
Battle	Blue
In	Indigo
Vain	Violet

Can you make up some other sayings to help you remember the order of the colors?

Make a Rainbow

Choose a sunny day for this experiment.

You will need:
- shallow bowl
- clean water
- small mirror
- white wall or big sheet of white paper

1 Place the bowl close to a sunny window.

2 Fill the bowl halfway with water.

3 Hold the mirror at an angle in the water.

4 Use the mirror to reflect a beam of sunlight onto the sheet of paper or wall.

5 Gently move the mirror in the water until you see a patch of rainbow on the paper or wall.

The sunlight traveling through the water has been split into all its separate colors.

Safety Note: *Do not look directly at the sun or shine the reflected sunlight from the mirror into your eyes.*

Try This!

Frost only forms when the temperature falls below freezing (32°F or 0°C), and usually when the nights are clear and there is no cloud cover in the sky.

Many countries have a fictional character named Jack Frost, who probably came from Scandinavian myths. When the ground is covered with frost, it is said there has been a visit from Jack Frost himself.

What do you think Jack Frost would look like? Draw a picture of him.

Frost

Frost can be as beautiful to look at as a rainbow. Frost is frozen dew. It is made up of tiny ice crystals that freeze into jewel-like patterns.

▲ *Thick frost is called hoar frost. It can be so thick that it looks like snow.*

Changing Weather

The world began about 4.6 billion years ago. World climates and weather have changed throughout the centuries. In the past, climates changed very gradually. But today scientists believe climates in all zones are changing more and more quickly. The whole world may be getting warmer.

Some scientists think that natural events may have caused these changes. They blame dust from volcanic eruptions and "wobbles" in the earth's orbit around the sun (*see page 11*).

⬆ *Burning fuels causes pollution.*

Did you know...

The El Niño effect is when warm sea currents flow into the usually cold Pacific Ocean, off the coast of Peru. These warm waters upset the normal temperatures in the air around the earth. They have an amazing "domino" effect on the world's weather. El Niño can cause floods in Australia and droughts in South Africa and can disturb weather patterns from Europe to Siberia.

El Niño means "the Christ child" in Spanish. It was given this name because it happens at Christmas time.

Air Pollution

Other scientists think that weather changes have been caused by people.

We need a lot of energy to live our lives today. We burn fuel, such as oil and coal, to provide the energy needed to power cars, trucks, planes, and ships. Factories, stores and power stations also burn many tons of fuel. Burning fuels gives off gases that pollute the air.

Trees naturally use up some of the gases that are given off when fuels are burned. But in some parts of the world, large areas of trees are cut down every day to make room to grow crops, graze cattle, and build houses.

Global Warming

Scientists believe all these changes can cause global warming. This is the gradual buildup of heat within the earth's atmosphere. Global warming may be affecting our weather.

Scientists check both natural changes and levels of pollution all the time to see what effects they have on the world's weather.

➤ *Data is fed back continually from radars and satellites to this control room so that meteorologists can monitor the weather.*

Try This! Weather Record

You can monitor the weather in your area by starting a long-term weather diary. Record what the weather is like twice a day. Write down the temperature, whether it is sunny or cloudy (*page 14*), or if it is raining (*page 17*).

Include in your diary a section for recording what the weather forecast is. Write down the forecast in the evening. Compare it with the weather you actually record the following day.

Date	Forecast	Temp°F	Rainfall	Weather
am				
pm				

Look through the national newspapers every week to see if there are any reports of weather disasters. Look back at your long-term weather report and see if any major changes in your local weather happened at the same time as the weather disaster.

Better Technology

With better and better technology, scientists can measure changes in the weather more accurately: spacecraft monitor the activity of the sun, specially equipped planes record data at the center of hurricanes, and floating weather stations gather information to try to predict such big changes in weather patterns as those caused by the El Niño effect.

What's More...

More Windy Things

Wind speed can be measured in a number of ways: miles or kilometers per hour, or in knots (one knot is 1 mph, or 1.85 kph). Another way to measure wind speed is to use the Beaufort scale. Sir Frances Beaufort was an admiral in the Royal Navy. He developed a system of measuring the force of wind for sailors to use. He divided wind speeds into 13 points.

Beaufort Scale

Force	mph	kph	Description	Effects on land
0	1	1	calm	smoke rises straight into air
1	2-3	1-5	light	air rising; smoke drifts slowly
2	4-7	6-11	light breeze	smoke shows direction of wind
3	8-12	12-19	gentle breeze	leaves and twigs move
4	13-18	20-29	moderate breeze	small branches move; paper blows around
5	19-24	30-38	fresh breeze	small, leafy trees sway
6	25-31	39-51	strong breeze	difficult to use umbrellas; large branches sway
7	32-38	51-61	near gale	difficult to walk into wind
8	39-46	62-74	gale	twigs snap off trees
9	47-54	75-86	strong gale	branches break; shingles blown off roofs
10	55-63	87-101	whole gale	trees uprooted
11	64-74	102-120	storm	cars overturned; trees blown some distance
12	over 74	over 120	hurricane	widespread destruction; buildings destroyed

Use the descriptions of the Beaufort scale to draw a picture chart of each stage.

Weather music

If you can play the recorder, try playing this piece of music taken from Antonio Vivaldi's (1678–1741) *The Four Seasons.*

Try This! Clothes for Climates

You will need: • thin cardboard • scissors • colored pencils or pens • books showing people in different parts of the world

1 Cut the thin cardboard into 24 pieces, about the same size and shape as playing cards.

2 Divide the cards into six sets of four cards, one set for the following climate zones: Mediterranean, polar, mountain, coastal, arid, and tropical.

3 From your resource books, find out as much as you can about the weather in these zones, and what people wear. You may like to work in a group, with each member finding out about a different climate zone.

4 Take one set of cards and decide which climate zone you will show.

mountain

5 Draw a head-covering suitable for that zone on one card, a suitable top or coat on another card, suitable trousers or skirt on the third card, and something suitable to wear on the feet on the last card. Write the climate zone on each card. When you have four cards for each climate zone, you are ready to play.

Get together with three or four friends. Collect all the cards and shuffle them. Pass them out equally.

You need to collect as many sets of cards as you can. Take turns to ask the other players if they have a card from a particular climate zone. For example, "Jo, do you have a top from a tropical zone?" If the player does have the card, they must give it to you and you can ask another question. If they do not have the card, that is the end of your turn.

The winner is the person who collects the most complete sets of cards.

Glossary

arid: dry. An arid climate is very dry, and usually hot in the daytime and cold at night.

atmosphere: the air that surrounds the earth.

average: a standard that is accepted as normal. For example, the average temperature of an area is the temperature that occurs most often in that area.

boiling point: the temperature at which a liquid turns into a gas. For example, water turns to water vapor at 212°F (100°C). This is the boiling point of water.

climate: the long-term weather pattern in a certain region or place.

combine: to join together.

continent: one of the seven main land-masses on the earth. These are Europe, Asia, Africa, North America and South America, Australia, and Antarctica.

cyclone: a violent, whirling wind.

droplets: very tiny drops.

freezing point: the temperature at which a liquid turns into a solid. For example, water turns to ice at 32°F (0°C). This is the freezing point of water.

generator: a machine that uses oil, coal, wind, or waves to make electricity.

global warming: the buildup of heat within the earth's atmosphere. It affects the world's weather. Many scientists believe that global warming is melting the icecaps in the polar regions.

hemisphere: the top half or bottom half of the earth.

hurricane: a dangerous tropical storm.

insulators: materials that do not allow heat or cold to pass through easily.

medieval: a period in history, from around A.D. 1000–1500.

meteorologist: a scientist who studies the weather.

orbit: the path of a planet, moon, or satellite in space.

Number Work Answers

page 6: The difference between 94°F (34.4°C) and -72°F (57.8°C) is 166°F (92.2°C).
The difference between 57.8°C) and -89.2°C (-128.6°F) is 264.6°F (147°C)

Glossary

pollution: unwanted or waste material that makes air, water, buildings, or land dirty. Noise and light can also cause pollution.

predict: to guess what will happen before it takes place.

radar: equipment that uses radio waves to find distant objects. It sends out radio waves and then records them as they bounce back. Radar can detect, or find, rain clouds.

satellite: a spacecraft containing scientific equipment that orbits the earth to record and send back information. Satellites record information about space and the weather on earth.

Scandinavian: from Scandinavia — the countries of Norway, Sweden, Denmark, and Finland, in Northern Europe.

seasons: changing weather patterns that happen at the same time each year.

subtropical: describes regions bordering the tropics where it is hot and fairly wet, with long, dry seasons.

temperate: a region in the world that has temperatures that are not often very hot or very cold.

tornado: a violent whirlwind.

tropical: describes regions close to the equator (an imaginary line around the middle of the earth) that have a hot and wet climate.

water vapor: water when it is a gas. Water turns from a liquid to a gas when it is heated.

waterlogged: covered with, and full of, water.

weather: the day-to-day changes in rain, sunshine, temperature, and wind.

weather stations: equipment used to give information about the weather. A weather station may be fixed, such as equipment stored in buildings and fields, or moving, such as satellites and balloons.

31

Index